HEROES OF BLACK HISTORY

FREDERICK DOUGLASS

BY JOAN STOLTMAN

Gareth Stevens PUBLISHING

Please visit our website, www.garethstevens.com. For a free color catalog of all our high-quality books, call toll free 1-800-542-2595 or fax 1-877-542-2596.

Library of Congress Cataloging-in-Publication Data

Names: Stoltman, Joan, author.
Title: Frederick Douglass / Joan Stoltman.
Description: New York : Gareth Stevens Publishing, [2019] | Series: Heroes of black history | Includes index.
Identifiers: LCCN 2018014476| ISBN 9781538230176 (library bound) | ISBN 9781538231296 (pbk.) | ISBN 9781538233092 (6 pack)
Subjects: LCSH: Douglass, Frederick, 1818-1895–Juvenile literature. | Slaves–United States–Biography–Juvenile literature. | Abolitionists–United States–Biography–Juvenile literature. | African American Fists–Biography–Juvenile literature. | Antislavery movements–United States–History–Juvenile literature. | African Americans–History–19th century–Juvenile literature.
Classification: LCC E449.D75 S76 2019 | DDC 973.8092 [B] –dc23
LC record available at https://lccn.loc.gov/2018014476

First Edition

Published in 2019 by
Gareth Stevens Publishing
111 East 14th Street, Suite 349
New York, NY 10003

Designer: Katelyn E. Reynolds
Editor: Joshua Turner

Photo credits: Cover, pp. 1 (Frederick Douglass), pp. 1–32 (background image), 14, 15, 19, 23, 25 courtesy of the Library of Congress; p. 5 Theshibboleth/Newfraferz87/Wikipedia.org; p. 7 Hulton Archive/Getty Images; p. 9 courtesy of the Library of Congress/Jayen466/Wikipedia.org; p. 11 (main) Smith Collection/Gado/Getty Images; p. 11 (inset) http://docsouth.unc.edu/neh/douglass/douglass.html/Quadell/Wikipedia.org; p. 13 Fotosearch/Getty Images; p. 16 Bettmann/Getty Images; p. 17 courtesy of the Library of Congress/Ser Amantio di Nicolao/Wikipedia.org; p. 20 Cowan's Auctions (https://www.cowanauctions.com/lot/men-of-color-to-arms-to-armsnow-or-never-exceptionally-rare-civil-war-recruitment-broadside-895225)/Scewing/Wikipedia.org; p. 21 Carol M. Highsmith/Buyenlarge/Getty Images; p. 27 MPI/Getty Images.

Printed in the United States of America

CPSIA compliance information: Batch #CW19GS: For further information contact Gareth Stevens, New York, New York at 1-800-542-2595.

CONTENTS

Words in the glossary appear in **bold** type the first time they are used in the text.

BORN A SLAVE

In 1818, Frederick Augustus Washington Bailey was born in Maryland. He was a slave and the property of Aaron Anthony. He later added the name Douglass and, despite his humble beginnings, became one of the greatest black leaders in American history.

At the age of 2, Frederick was taken from his mother, after which point he rarely saw her. His grandmother raised him until he began work at Anthony's home when he was only 6 years old. Anthony was mean to his slaves. He beat Frederick and made him sleep in the kitchen closet. Frederick's older sister, Eliza, taught him how to survive. When Anthony died, Frederick became the property of Anthony's daughter, Lucretia.

SLAVERY IN AMERICA

American slaves had no rights and served their owners for life. At birth, the children of slaves became the property of their parents' owners. Children were often separated from their mothers at birth or soon after, just as Frederick was. Families were often broken up further as members were bought and sold as property throughout their lives.

UNITED STATES, 1821

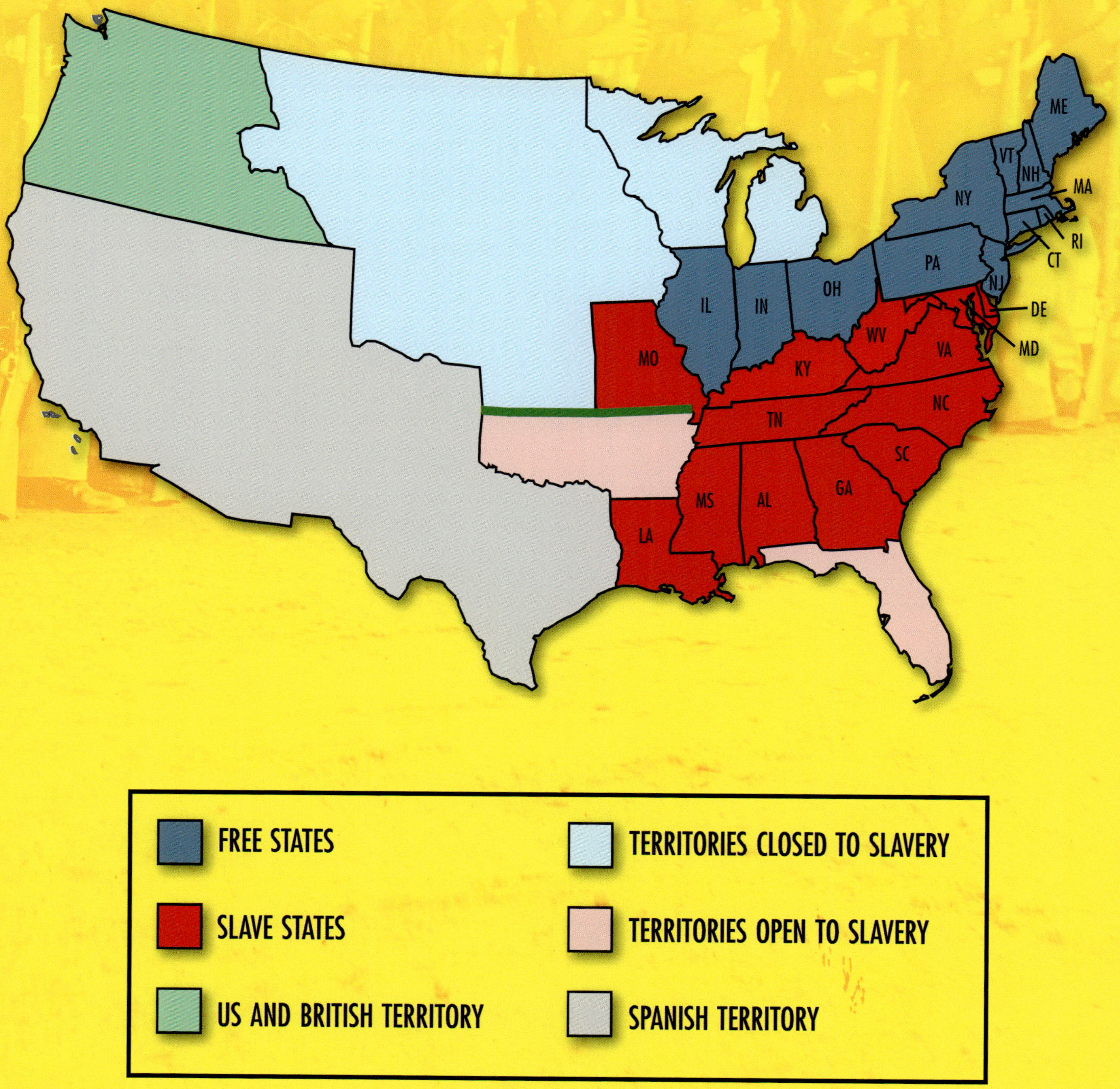

By 1821, the United States was divided between states and territories that allowed slavery and those that didn't.

When he was 10 years old, Frederick was sent to Lucretia's family in Baltimore, Maryland. The lady of the house, Sophia Auld, had never owned a slave. She treated Frederick with respect and even taught him the alphabet—until her husband angrily put an end to it. Focused on learning how to read, Frederick continued teaching himself.

Upon Lucretia's death, Frederick became the property of her husband. When Frederick was caught teaching other slaves to read, he was sent to a slave breaker, a master who beats slaves to make them listen and behave. One day, Frederick decided that he had had enough, and he fought back. He was never beaten again.

SLAVE CODES

Slave codes were laws designed to keep slaves in their place. Not only was it illegal for slaves to read or write, it was also illegal for someone to teach a slave to do so. Slaves weren't even allowed to own books. They couldn't gather, marry, or travel without a white person's permission.

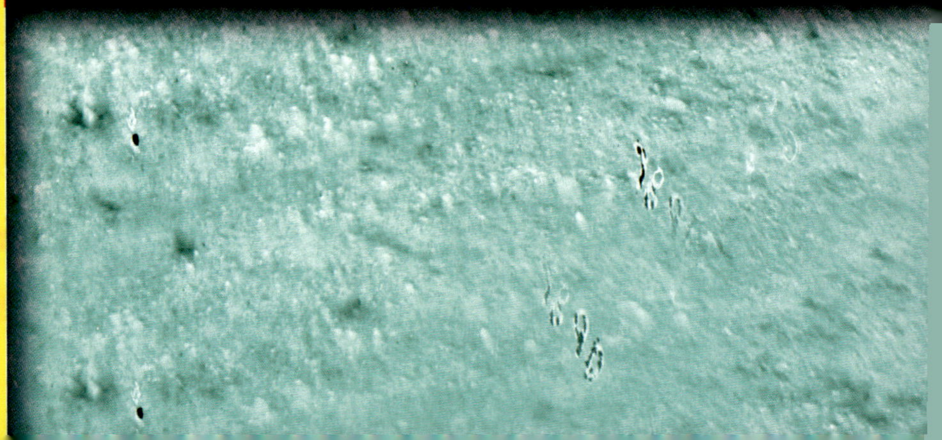

Life was very different for Frederick when he lived in Baltimore. In cities, slaves were commonly better fed and clothed. They were often allowed to move more freely, although they were still subject to the slave codes.

FREDERICK'S GREAT ESCAPE

After he stood up to the slave breaker, Frederick vowed to escape. He tried and failed to escape in 1836. He was jailed for his escape attempt, and then he was sent to work in a shipyard in Baltimore. There he met a free black housekeeper named Anna Murray, who made him a sailor's uniform and gave him money to escape.

On September 3, 1838, Frederick, who was just age 20, traveled by train and steamboat to New York, a free state. Several times during the trip, he was almost discovered. Eleven days later, Anna and Frederick were married, and they both took a new last name: Douglass.

ALL IN THE DETAILS

While there were laws against, and harsh penalties for, helping a slave to escape, many people were still willing to try. A free black sailor lent Frederick his identification papers so Frederick could pretend to be free. The sailor could have been jailed or killed if Frederick had been caught or if the sailor had needed his papers to prove his own freedom while Frederick still had them.

Anna Murray Douglass

Frederick didn't tell the whole story of his escape until 1881. This was to protect Anna and the others who helped him.

AFTER THE ESCAPE

Frederick and Anna joined the **thriving** free black community of New Bedford, Massachusetts. He worked as a **laborer**, trained as a preacher, and attended **abolitionist** meetings. At one such meeting in 1841, he decided to tell some of his life story. His training as a preacher had prepared him well to speak in front of crowds, and soon he began touring the North as an abolitionist speaker.

In 1845, Douglass wrote an **autobiography**. Although the book became famous, it also put him at risk of being captured and returned to slavery. Douglass escaped to Great Britain for 2 years, where his story touched abolitionists so much that they collected enough funds to purchase his freedom—over $21,000 in today's money!

THE REALITY OF SLAVERY

Douglass was one of the first escaped slaves to tell his story. The horrors he both spoke and wrote about shocked many, even abolitionist audiences. Although his speeches and writings brought many followers to the movement, he angered white Northerners who, despite where they lived, truly believed that blacks should be slaves. He was attacked in the North many times for speaking out against slavery.

NARRATIVE

OF THE

LIFE

OF

FREDERICK DOUGLASS,

AN

AMERICAN SLAVE.

WRITTEN BY HIMSELF.

BOSTON:
PUBLISHED AT THE ANTI-SLAVERY OFFICE,
No. 25 CORNHILL
1845.

Through his 1845 autobiography, *Narrative of the Life of Frederick Douglass, an American Slave*, and his other writing and speeches, Douglass repeatedly presented the violence and nonstop horrors of slavery. He did this to show people that slavery needed to end as quickly as possible.

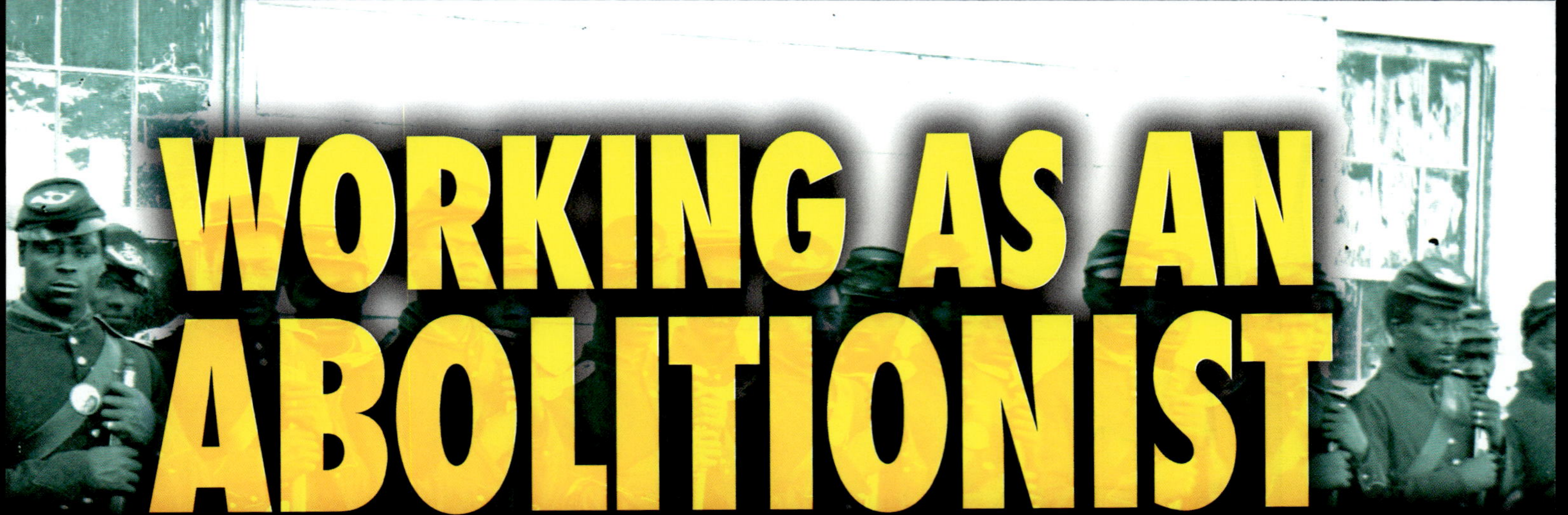

WORKING AS AN ABOLITIONIST

Many people thought that Douglass's autobiography could not have been written by a black person. When he spoke, they claimed that he was too well-spoken to have been a slave. They couldn't shake off their beliefs and feelings about race.

Douglass worked hard to prove their **racism** wrong and show that blacks were deserving of freedom and respect. He examined scientific claims "proving" whites were naturally better than other races so that he could pull apart their arguments and prove that blacks and whites were equal. Douglass even pointed out the **contradiction** of a country being founded on justice and freedom, yet allowing slavery. He made people question their worldviews and beliefs.

THE ABOLITIONISTS

Many white Northerners didn't think blacks could be educated or become part of society. Even Douglass's fellow abolitionists were capable of holding racist beliefs. The famous senator Henry Clay agreed that slavery wasn't **morally** right but also thought that abolition went too far because the southern economy depended on slavery. He and others proposed returning all blacks to Africa!

On July 5, 1852, Douglass gave one of his most famous speeches. He spoke about the contradiction of celebrating Independence Day in a country where slavery still exists.

WORKING AS A BLACK ABOLITIONIST

William Lloyd Garrison was the leader of the abolitionist movement and an early supporter of Douglass. Garrison didn't believe in voting or political parties. In contrast, as Douglass learned more about politics, he came to believe they were the key to abolition. Garrison thought the North should separate from the South, but that would leave Douglass's family members still enslaved in the South. When Douglass spoke about Northern racism, Garrison felt it took focus away from the abolitionist cause. But Douglass knew that racism allowed slavery to continue existing.

By 1851, in an important moment for the abolitionist movement in America, Douglass formally parted ways with Garrison.

THE BLACK ABOLITIONISTS

Because there were not many free blacks, there were not many black abolitionists. Black abolitionists knew what was at stake and didn't have time for planning or **compromise**. More importantly, their experiences with racism in the North showed them that they also needed equal rights laws immediately. This was frightening to white people in both the North and the South.

William Lloyd Garrison, founder of the American Anti-Slavery Society (AASS)

Racism in Northern states meant free blacks couldn't vote, own property, travel freely, or get a good education. Black abolitionists built their own communities, churches, and antislavery organizations in order to serve their own specific needs.

SUPPORTING WOMEN'S RIGHTS

Douglass firmly believed in equality for all, and he practiced this in many ways, most notably with his strong support for the women's rights movement. In fact, each issue of his newspaper, *The North Star,* said this: "Right is of no Sex—Truth is of no Color." Furthermore, he often spoke about how **sexism** and racism were related.

In 1848, Douglass was the only African American to attend the first women's rights convention in Seneca Falls, New York. There he spoke about how all people should have the right to vote. Long after slavery ended, he continued to fight for equal rights for women and blacks.

THE RAILROAD

Douglass became part of the Underground Railroad, too. The Underground Railraod was a secret way for slaves to escape to freedom in the North and Canada. People called conductors helped the escaped slaves make their way to safe houses, called stations. The Underground Railroad had many routes, or lines, and traveling all of them was difficult and dangerous for both the slaves and those who helped them.

women's rights convention in Seneca Falls, NY

THE NORTH STAR.

RIGHT IS OF NO SEX—TRUTH IS OF NO COLOR—GOD IS THE FATHER OF US ALL, AND ALL WE ARE BRETHREN.

VOL. I. NO. 23.

ROCHESTER, N. Y., FRIDAY, JUNE 2, 1848.

WHOLE NO.—23.

Communication.

Selections.

From 1847 to 1860, Douglass ran an abolitionist newspaper called *The North Star,* and later *Frederick Douglass' Paper.* He often wrote about racism in America and women's rights, and he reported on abolitionist issues.

THE BRINK OF WAR

Abolitionist leader John Brown believed that a violent overthrow would end slavery. Over the years, Douglass had argued with Brown that violence would make racism worse and would push the country further from the abolitionist position. In 1859, Brown attempted a violent overthrow of slavery in Harpers Ferry, Virginia. In the aftermath, letters from Douglass were found among Brown's belongings, and Douglass was wanted in connection with Brown. This caused Douglass to flee the country.

In 1857, the Supreme Court, the highest court in the United States, had ruled that blacks, even free blacks, had no rights and were not citizens. This meant that Douglass could not travel outside the country. He had to obtain special paperwork from France and remain in Europe for 5 months until his name was cleared.

CAUSES OF THE WAR

Most Northerners did not care about slavery but feared the South having more political power. Meanwhile, Southerners felt that their way of life was under attack. After Abraham Lincoln was elected president in 1860, Southern states left the Union one by one to form the Confederate States of America. This was an effort to protect their economic interests and uphold the institution of slavery.

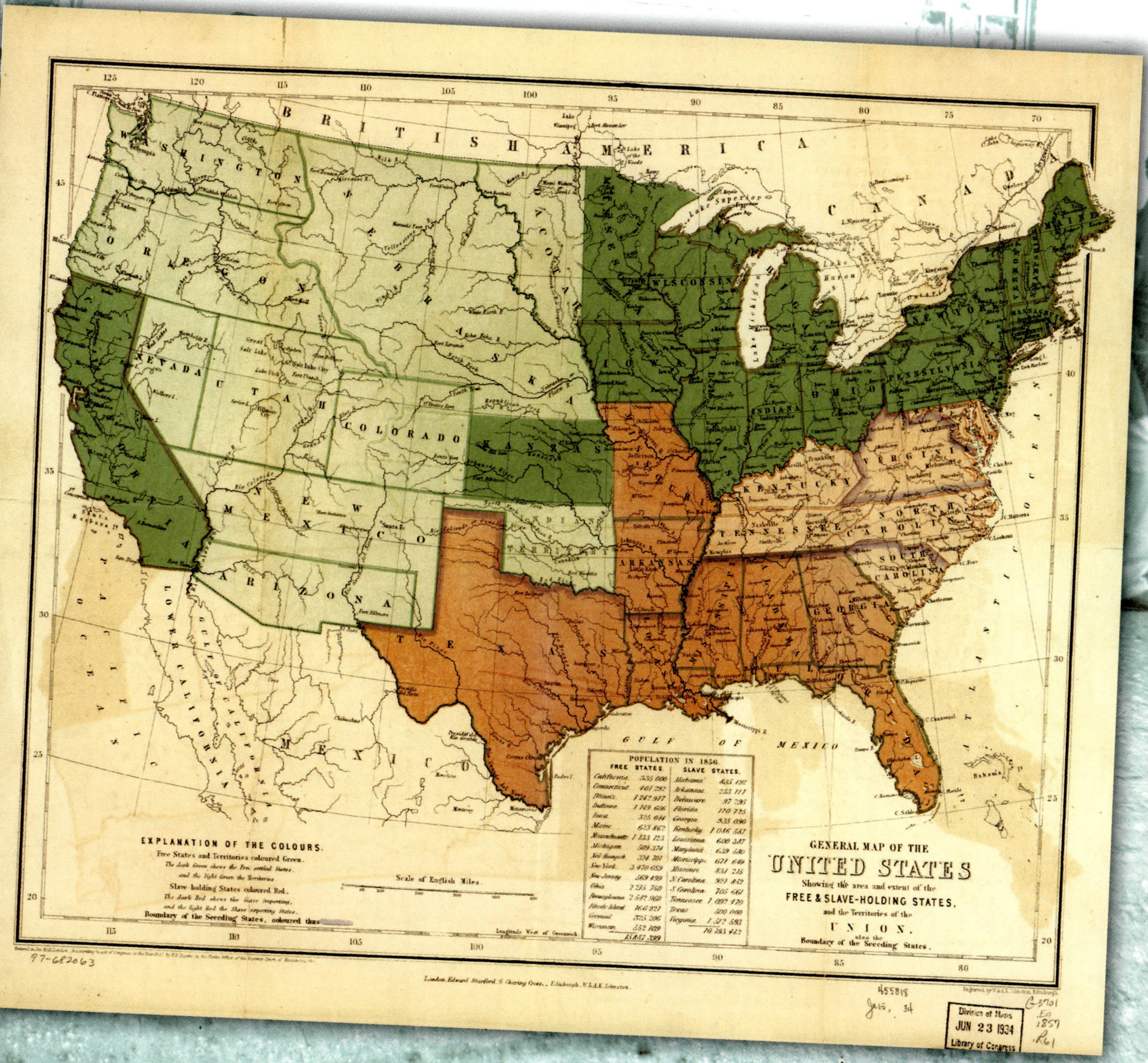

Throughout the 1850s, there was a battle for control of the federal government. Land out west was being made into new states, and that meant new seats were being added to Congress. The South wanted to fill Congress with people who supported slavery, and the North was concerned that more slave states would tip the balance of power.

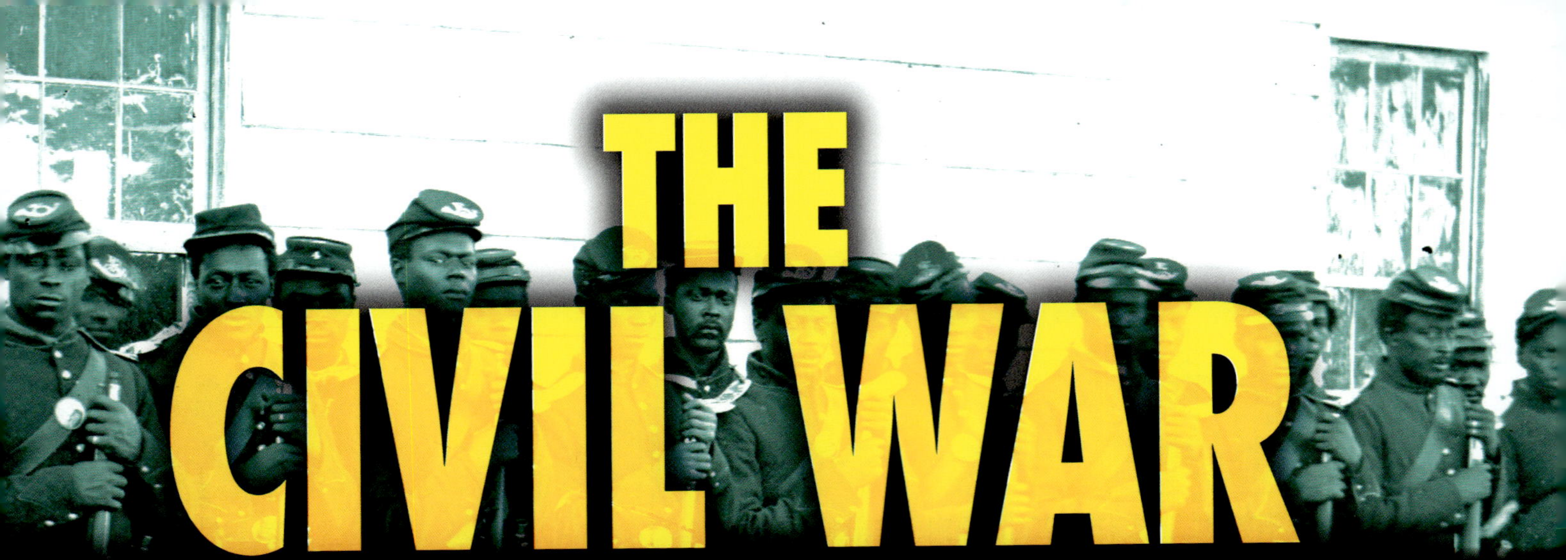

THE CIVIL WAR

Douglass saw in the Civil War a potential end to slavery, and he fought hard throughout it to help the North win. He met with President Lincoln several times, urging him to declare the war a fight against slavery and to let blacks fight. But, for the first few years, Lincoln did neither.

In 1863, about 2 years into the war, Lincoln issued the Emancipation Proclamation, which both allowed blacks to fight and focused the war more on ending slavery. Douglass helped black men to sign up to fight, and over 186,000 black men served, including three of his sons. He met with Lincoln to argue for better supplies and pay for black soldiers.

EMANCIPATION PROCLAMATION

The Emancipation Proclamation declared slaves in Confederate states free partly because the Union needed more soldiers. This wasn't the freedom abolitionists wanted. They wanted the country and its president to choose moral justice for blacks. But Douglass continued supporting Lincoln because he believed that he could convince him to pass equal rights laws.

Civil War recruitment poster

Douglass did not like Lincoln at first, because Lincoln wouldn't commit to abolition. But Douglass came to realize that Lincoln was doing what he could to keep the Union together, and Douglass grew to respect and understand him.

AFTER THE WAR

When the Thirteenth Amendment passed in 1865 and slavery was made illegal, Garrison announced the abolitionist movement a success. Douglass and other black abolitionists disagreed. Their cause didn't end when slavery ended because blacks didn't yet have equal rights under the law.

Douglass saw this period as a chance for a rebirth of the country. The Constitution changed a lot in the next few years, and he spoke publicly about each change. He opposed the Fourteenth Amendment in 1868 because it didn't protect the right to vote. He fought for the Fifteenth Amendment because it protected black men's voting rights, but this angered the women's rights advocates because it did not grant voting rights to women.

EARLY CHANGES

In the early years after the Civil War ended, there were many attempts to undo the effects of slavery on politics and society. The Enforcement Act of 1871 allowed the military to be used against racist groups like the Ku Klux Klan, and the Civil Rights Act of 1875 banned **discrimination** in public places.

In 1865, Congress established the Freedmen's Bureau to help former slaves find jobs and housing. It also funded black hospitals and schools.

Now an important black leader in Washington, DC, Douglass often met with the president to give his opinion or to push for action on an issue. He worked with five presidents after Lincoln on equal rights and **access** for blacks and women, among other causes. He was even nominated for president!

Douglass continued speaking on a wide range of issues, even unpopular ones. One of his opinions that was especially unpopular was his displeasure that blacks were isolating themselves into communities separate from whites.

In 1864, Douglass made his first trip back to Maryland, the state of his birth and slave life. He later took several more trips and even met with his former owner.

THE FREEDMAN'S BANK

After the war, Congress created the Freedman's Savings and Trust Company especially for former slaves as a way for them to safely store their money. When it began to fail, Douglass took over the company, but it couldn't be saved. Congress refused to return any money, and many hopes of a better life after slavery were lost.

The member records of the Freedman's Savings and Trust Company are still used today to fill in family trees, as they are the largest list of former slaves ever made by one group.

AFTER RECONSTRUCTION

Douglass was the first black person to hold a high government position when he became marshal of Washington, DC, in 1877. He continued to work for the government in many positions until 1891. After the death of his wife, Anna, he married Helen Pitts, a young, white, women's rights **activist** who was the daughter of an abolitionist friend. Their marriage was often attacked.

Racism was never truly gone from life in the United States. Douglass became a powerful activist against discrimination laws called black codes, which were being passed in the South. Violence against blacks in the 1890s was fierce, but Douglass remained hopeful for the future of his country and his people.

BLACK CODES

Blacks soon lost their protections under the law again. An entire system of discriminatory state laws called black codes was established throughout the South. These laws were meant to keep former slaves from succeeding in the South. Some states didn't allow black people to own certain property or hold certain jobs. These laws lasted until the civil rights movement of the 1960s, and their effects are still felt today.

In Douglass's last autobiography, *Life and Times of Frederick Douglass,* he wrote about his great concern for where the country was headed. He also looked back on his life's work proudly.

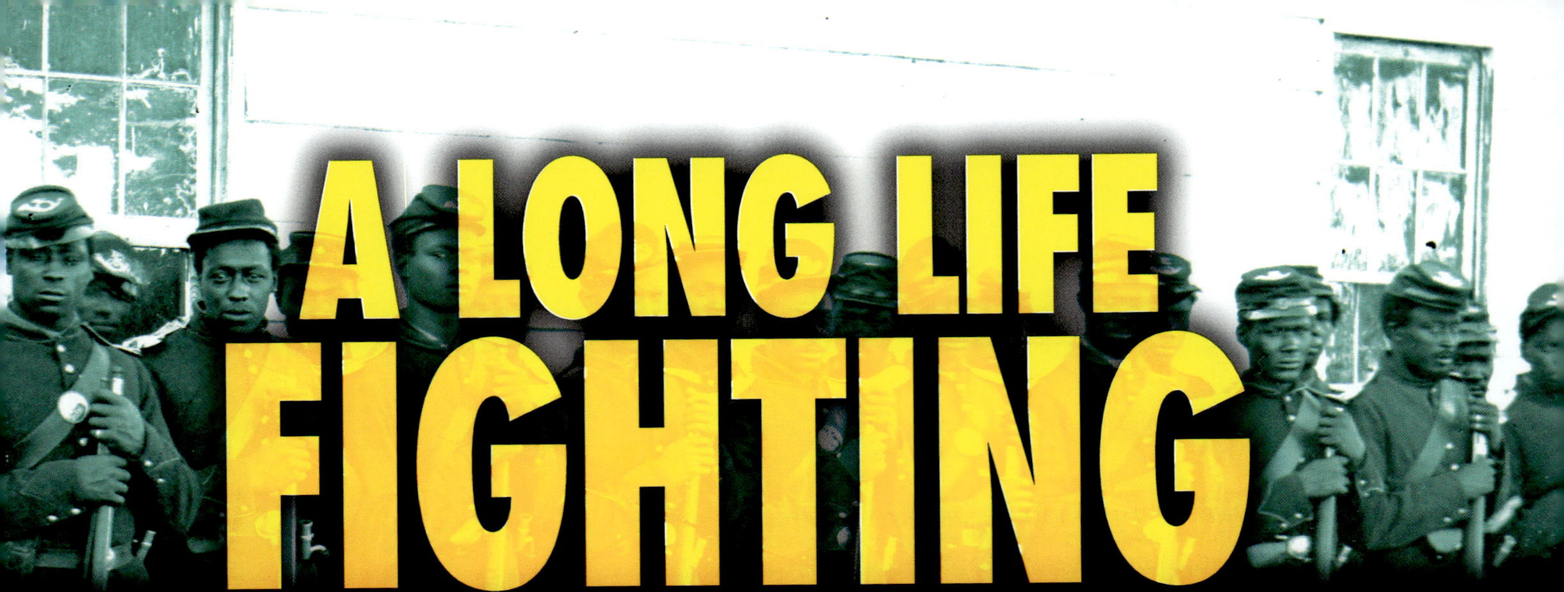

A LONG LIFE FIGHTING

Frederick Douglass died on February 20, 1895, a few hours after he delivered a speech that brought listeners to their feet at a meeting of the National Council of Women. Thousands attended his funeral. Women's rights activist Susan B. Anthony gave a speech written by fellow activist Elizabeth Cady Stanton honoring their friend.

Douglass is forever remembered as one of the first black leaders in American history. He believed in his country and in the equality of all people. He took the role of being a voice for black Americans very seriously, and he worked tirelessly every day to speak on behalf of those who could not speak for themselves.

MILLIONS OF WORDS

Douglass wrote thousands of speeches and articles that are still read today and are used by activists to inspire change. His autobiographies are some of the most important books in American history. His writing is a record of how he witnessed 77 years of the most important and turbulent period in American history.

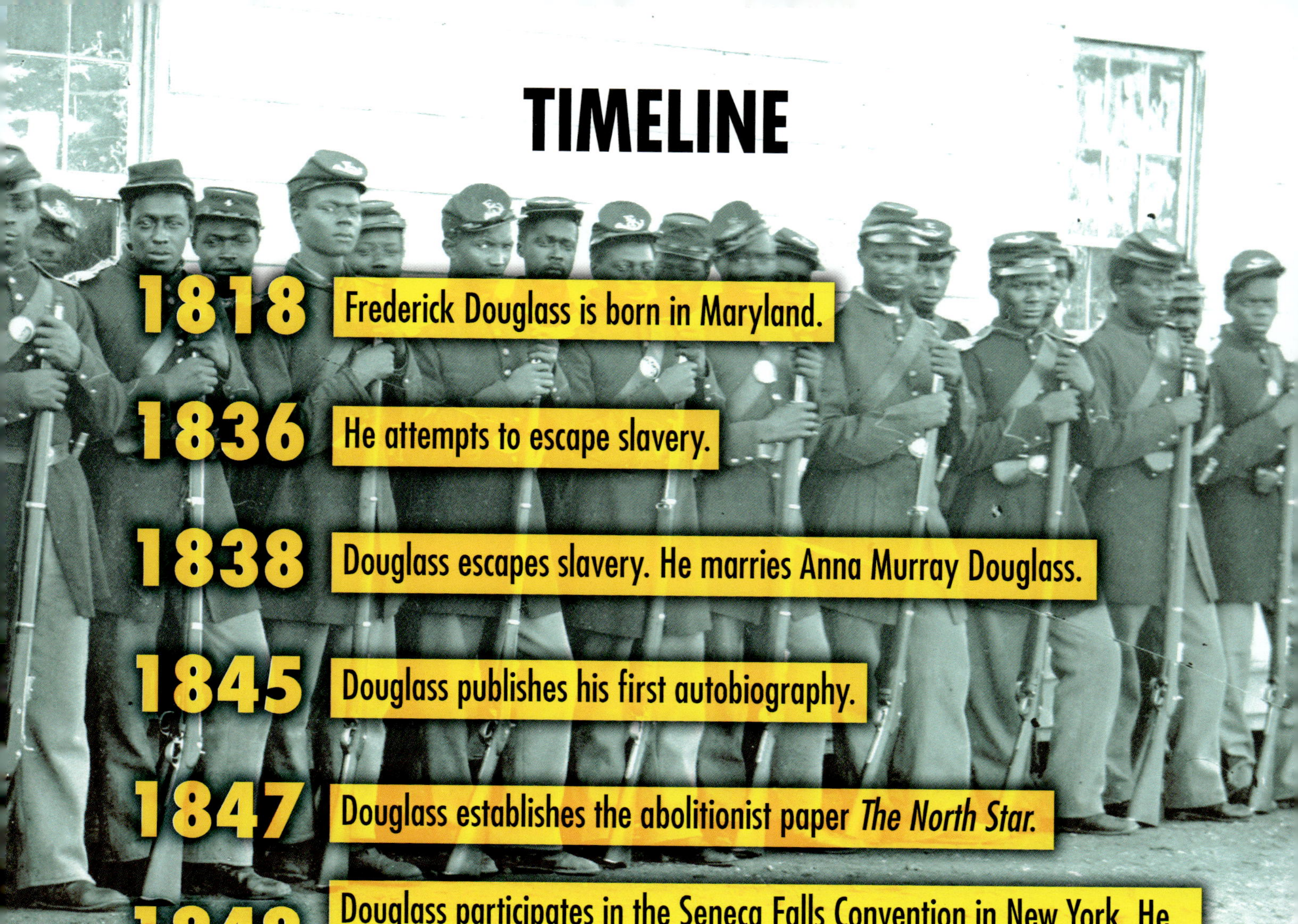

TIMELINE

1818 Frederick Douglass is born in Maryland.

1836 He attempts to escape slavery.

1838 Douglass escapes slavery. He marries Anna Murray Douglass.

1845 Douglass publishes his first autobiography.

1847 Douglass establishes the abolitionist paper *The North Star*.

1848 Douglass participates in the Seneca Falls Convention in New York. He begins working with the Underground Railroad to help escaped slaves.

1855 Douglass publishes his second autobiography.

1874 He becomes president of Freedman's Savings and Trust Company.

1877 Douglass is appointed US Marshal of Washington, DC.

1881 He publishes his third autobiography, *Life and Times of Frederick Douglass*.

1895 Frederick Douglass dies.

GLOSSARY

abolitionist: one who fights to end slavery

access: the right to enter, get near, or make use of something, or to have contact with someone

activist: a person who uses or supports strong actions to help make changes in politics or society

autobiography: a book written by someone about their own life

compromise: a way of two sides reaching an agreement in which each gives up something to end an argument

contradiction: a difference between two things that indicates that both cannot be true

discrimination: unfairly treating people unequally because of their race, beliefs, or other identifying characteristics

laborer: a person who does hard physical work for money

morally: having to do with what is right or wrong

racism: the belief that people of different races have different qualities and abilities and that some races are superior or inferior

sexism: unfair treatment of people because of their sex, especially unfair treatment of women

thriving: growing or developing successfully

FOR MORE INFORMATION

BOOKS

Cline-Ransome, Lesa. *Words Set Me Free: The Story of Young Frederick Douglass.* New York, NY: Simon & Schuster Books for Young Readers, 2012.

Gregory, Josh. *Frederick Douglass.* New York, NY: Children's Press, 2016.

Kramer, Barbara. *Frederick Douglass.* Washington, DC: National Geographic, 2017.

WEBSITES

Famous Abolitionists
www.socialstudies.com/pdf/SPL116A.pdf
Print this activity book all about abolition and the abolitionists.

Frederick Douglass' Paper
nyheritage.org/collections/frederick-douglass-paper
See real pages of *Frederick Douglass' Paper,* which was printed from 1851 to 1860.

The North Star
nyheritage.org/collections/north-star
Check out pages of *The North Star,* the abolitionist newspaper Douglass printed from 1847 to 1851.

Virtual Tour
www.nps.gov/frdo/learn/photosmultimedia/virtual-tour.htm
If you can't visit Washington, DC, to see the Frederick Douglass National Historic Site, go here to take two different online tours!

Publisher's note to educators and parents: Our editors have carefully reviewed these websites to ensure that they are suitable for students. Many websites change frequently, however, and we cannot guarantee that a site's future contents will continue to meet our high standards of quality and educational value. Be advised that students should be closely supervised whenever they access the internet.

INDEX